MAGI

MAGI

D'Griot

D'griot

For myself, Of Sun and Moon, and the pursuit of belonging with my ancestors

1

Divergence

Divergence
A desire met with unrest
One to the shining stars
One to the pits of the abyss
One a journey up the Etz Hayim
One a battle through the Qlippoth
Both Equal in their own right

2

Royal

Royal
The Winds blow towards Royalty
An Aspect that is cultivated
And Matched
By divinity
To form
A
Genuine Trinity
Where the bearer of the crown
Is reflected by the force above

3

Preface

Preface : The dimensions of Studying or the Notary Art

1. The First Dimension: Completion
    1. The use of numbers and decimals to make a topic of study complete
2. The Second Dimension: Details
    1. Identifying what parts are principles and what parts are details
3. Third dimension: Essays
    1. Writing Essays on the principles for better understanding
4. Fourth Dimension: Practice
    1. Practice and Memorization of a Topic

4

Table of Contents

Table of contents

5

The Way of Ish

- The Child's Universe is where a being creates itself using the Yin energy provided by the Goddess and the Yang energy provided by the God-Father. In creation a being choose what will be its ultimate form and works within the child Universe on that Goal. It is through these laws and the way that the Great Spirit Speaks. Ish means: through this, the Spirit of God will listen.
- The two part goal of Ish
    - The arrow of creation
        1. Existence
        2. Bliss
        3. Consciousness
        4. Commitment to the divine
    - The keys of creation
        1. Attainment and mastery of Key 0- The fool
        2. Attainment and mastery of Key 1- The magician
        3. Attainment and mastery of key 2- The priest

4. Attainment and mastery of Key 3- The divine Feminine
5. Attainment and mastery of Key 4- The Emperor

- The work of Ish is working on the keys and becoming a Magical Emperor able to end the suffering of others.This work will take centuries.
- The divine mother represents the Divine freedom offered in the universe. The divine Father represents the Divine Order in the Universe. When combined, they create a school in the Child's Universe
- The four laws that creates the way
    - Law 1: A being in the kingdom of the lord consists of Spirit and Soul. The spirit is a child of the Eternal Father and the soul is a child of the Eternal Mother.
    - Law 2: There are two principles that govern the Universe. The magnetic water (Yin) principle and the electric Fire (yang) principle. The Yin principle is responsible for physicality and form. The Yang principle is responsible for the infinite energy of Spirit. A third principle known as source originates these two principles.
    - Law 3: There are three natures in the Universe.
        - Order
        - Flow and Balance
        - Chaos
    - Law 4:
        - The whole development of beings lead towards mastery, flow and balance of these two principles
- The Way: A blissful being comes about when a being has understanding and state of contentment of the six directions (which are infinite)
    - The Upper World
    - The Underworld

- The self
- The other
- The past
- The future

Premier: The Law of the Way

- The Premier to the law states that the natural state of the universe oscillates between order and chaos. Chaos is simply an absence of order, and order an absence of Chaos. As such mastery comes from training and living in the natural state of the universe. The way is actualized when the three bodies are simultaneously aspire towards the way.
    - Physical: Transmutation of pain into Pleasure
    - Soul: Transmute depression into happiness
    - Spirit: Transmute darkness into light

* As such a savior is any who is able to transmute in such a way
Rituals of the Law

- Ritual 0: Acknowledging the Dream-like nature of Existence and actualizing your internal, individual and unique power and existence
- Ritual 1: Striving for mastery of your existence by flowing between order and chaos. The process of gaining objective spiritual power
- Ritual 2: Practice of the gift of creation. Actualizing through the way. The achievement of Immortality

6

Downwards and Upwards

7

Downwards and Upwards

Downwards and upwards: A case for a shadow spirituality towards light

1. The nature of Illumination
    1. The past as a book
    2. First Arts: Observation and Memory as an Effort to Understand the Name and Shape of Things
2. The being star and the Story Star
    1. God's ladder
    2. The Staircase of the Goddess
    3. Tree of Life
3. A general theory of the state of Malkuth
4. The dimensions of Malkuth
5. The Fire way of Knowing and the Water way of Knowing
6. The five essential yogas of a magi and their medium
    1. Kriya and Karma
        1. Kriya Yoga

   2. Bhakti Yoga
   3. Karma Yoga
   4. Jnana Yoga
   5. Tantra Yoga
7. Royalty and A vessel : A crown as the perfect vessel
8. The Lord and the Shadow of Malkuth: Its many forms, elemental and beyond
9. A pursuit towards a downwards Shadow spirituality in finding divinity

8

The nature of illumination

The nature of Illumination

The past as a book

Man after all his basic needs are met desire to know, it is why we have recreation and outlets for experience, schools,news,and civilization.We start with battling with the first principles of things and go from there, we have a belief and battle with it until we know, The nature of belief has shown me that possibility and education goes hand in hand. If we want a better world we should focus on a positive system of education that fosters a study of the past, cultivates an appreciation for knowledge and nature so that we can expand possibility.

Education ideally is supposed to make you a better person and a stronger producer of knowledge. Metaphysics has taught me that with the right foundations, one can wield truth like a light to find more truth. It has also taught me that without the right foundations, finding truth becomes like an obstacle course or arena in which you are not well equipped. A good education is important because it acts as a system of initiation where we develop warriors of truth, and most importantly a good education puts one in the position where he can find and develop new knowledge. Dorothy Sayers holds that a great defect in our education is that "although we often succeed in teaching our pupils 'subjects,' we fail lamentably on the whole in teaching" how to think (Sayers 604). Our current education thinks of subjects as something existing in detachment of other subjects, when in fact a good education teaches the interconnectivity of knowledge because it should be built on a strong foundation that everything is added. Metaphysics offers a solid foundation of learning any other subjects because it studies what all other subjects have to stand on, Reality.

We often like to think that we know what is true or not but as humans living in the vastness of the universe, we should not count anything out of our belief system as being outside the realms of truth. We can define truth as being an accurate characterization of reality. It is important that we are able to recognize truth because without recognizing it, we do not know if we have knowledge. A key component of acquiring knowledge is belief. Now I believe that belief is an important and powerful tool that humans possess. Belief is a mental characterization of reality. A negative aspect of belief is that someone can believe something that is far from an accurate characterization of reality, but this is also a positive aspect of belief because it sets us up as humans for growth. For example, the belief that "humans could roam the sky like the birds do" in a time before airplanes can be seen as outlandish to the people who do not hold the belief because it is so far from the truth. This belief, however, becomes less outlandish as someone makes that belief truth and acquires the knowledge of how to make humans roam the skies like the birds.Using the law of analogy, something as outlandish in our present condition, such as world peace or an end to world hunger being possible is in the realm of belief. The fact that we can hold this belief allows us to reach for the stars and make it a reality.

The past is a beautiful book of mysteries and wonder and studying it is much more beneficial than planning for the future. The future is like a single page while the past is a cover with many pages. On the topic of persistence, it is important to think about what survives changes as we cycle from past to present to future.I most like the view of Perdurantism in which we "view that objects persist over time by being spread out or extended over it (Ney 173)". Objects are four-dimensional and they spread out in time in the same way they spread out in space. I would like to add to this and say that ideas do the same thing as well. Going off of this, I would say that ideas are four-dimensional and more durable than physical objects. For example, we can think of the many ways in which ideas can be preserved. An idea can be written down, it can be analyzed through events, and it can be passed down by word of mouth. A unique thing about ideas that separate it from a concrete physical object is that while a physical object can persist throughout time, if it is destroyed, it being a particular thing is destroyed forever (unless we develop time travel and recover the object). An idea, however, can pop up throughout time even after being destroyed. It is common sense to believe that two people can believe the same thing, or have the same idea without ever interacting because, in order to have an idea, you just have to have a mental characterization of reality.Let us hold that that the more persistent an idea, the better it is at spanning that four-dimensional measurement we call time. I take value in myth, stories, and history because when looking at these mediums of ideas we start to see patterns that show that certain ideas and themes are not only crucial to humanity but have been with us for a very long time.

I think that knowledge and nature go hand in hand because nature is very persistent in its temporal component, at least when it comes to its laws. We can think about how our ancestors used to have access to the persistence of ideas without the written word. How did they find knowledge without the book of the past? Another book we have in gaining knowledge is the book of nature. We can see many themes that stand out in nature;themes of survival, differences, love, conflict, and peace. It has many laws that the ancients used to apply to themselves so that they can better co-exist with it.The persistence of nature is how we got many of the natural sciences and it is where the fundamental lessons of stability and co-existence are ever-so-present. It is up to us to learn from it but as Wendell Berry explains in *It All Turns on Affection* "human life has become less creaturely and more engineered, less familiar and more remote from local places,resources, pleasures, and associations ". He claims that our knowledge has become more statistical and in my view, we are no longer living on a book that nature is, but a page created by us; A page that can easily tear. But we are optimists that hold the belief that there is hope because it is in our belief that forces us to find knowledge on making and adjusting our reality.

Man has many books we can learn from but in order to begin to learn from them, one must have a good foundation of thinking which is the duty of school and education. An education should show the interconnectivity of things, it should also show the importance of things and how to differentiate a book from a single page. When we are able to differentiate from these two ideas we can add to it and progress.

9

First Arts

First Arts: Observation and Memory as an Effort to Understand the Name and Shape of Things

Observation is an art and Memory is also an art. These can be considered the first two arts we have to master as we will be using it for the rest of our lives and in all aspects of our lives. Understanding is the Domain of Wisdom and it takes time, Learning is the Domain of Knowledge and it takes effort and structure. In order to lead to a deeper understanding of things, we have to create a framework so that we can see where we are going. We must first differentiate between knowing the name of a thing and knowing the shape of a thing and differentiate between an object and art. We can say that Observation is finding the name of a thing, and memory is filling in its shape.

Names and Shapes

The difference between knowing a name and shape is that to know the name of a thing is to know part of it from one viewpoint. We gather names of things from various viewpoints in order to find a shape of it. To know the shape of something is a kind of spiritual task as to know the shape of a thing is to know it fully, from all perspectives and how it connects to everything. Names help form the shape of a thing.

Difference between an Object and an Art

The difference between an Object and an Art is that one has the focus of Observation (Object) and the other has the focus of Production (Art). Art is an extension of an object with the purpose of producing that object. All objects have names, some names are more complex than others, and object name may exist in other domains and dimensions than the apparent dimension. One key term here is an Arcanum; An Arcanum has magical connotations that we will eventually explore. But essentially an Arcanum is finding these complex names and arts in order to better understand and manipulate and produce objects. An Arcanum is a formula if I could use the correct term.

Observation and Memory as an Art

Observation: Observation as art has the end goal of finding a comprehensible shape of a thing/object through various means. The main one is finding the names of that thing from all different perspectives.

Memory: Memory as an Art has the end goal of filling the shape of an object that you already have. Understanding it more fully so that it becomes part of you.

The being star and the story Star

Two fundamental aspects of describing reality is through the being star and the Story star. The being star is a three dimensional representation of reality of awareness. The story star is a four dimensional representation of the reality of awareness. These two tools are tools of observation and memory to discern the shape and names of things. They are also a 0th key to understanding reality.

The being star

The origin of the being star is a star that is formed from joining two opposite forces together; An expansive force that is represented by an upwards triangle, an a contracting force that is represented by a downwards triangle. These two triangles represent the two original forces in creation of this earthly plane. The expansive triangle can be thought to represent creative power, and the downward triangle can be thought of as the destructive power. When the two forces get balance we get an equilibrium that is the equilibrium of being. The balancing force of these two original forces is known as the equilibrium force. The force that makes the manifested universe is known as the manifesting force. In traditional magic, these forces have names

1. Expansive force: Fire
2. Contractive force: Water
3. Equilibrium force: Air
4. Manifesting force : Earth

The force or energy that creates all of these forces and is present in all of them is known as the force of origin. In magic this force or energy is known as the Akashic Principle. This force can also be considered to be the force of God, or the Great Spirit.

When the being star is constructed we can use it as a guide to understand the manifested Universe

Story star

The story star is an alternative form of the Being Star. While the being star is used to understand three dimensional being, the story star is used to represent a four dimensional being. The elements of the being star are of a higher nature. The force that creates the four dimensional world is Time. The force that Limits the four dimensional world is space. The force that gives these two forces a sort of flow is Story. The force that solidifies these elements is known as actuality. The four dimensional story star allows everything to be possible as long as these four elements combine correctly. The force that gives origin to actuality is also the akashic principle or the Great Spirit

1. Fire: Time
2. Water: Space
3. Air: Story
4. Earth: Actuality

10

Understanding the World above and below

Understanding world above and the world below

The being star and the story star are crucial for understanding and constructing magical matrices; God's Ladder and the StairCase of the Goddess. God's Ladder and The staircase of the Goddess are two important ideas in constructing the universal Tree of Life.

God's Ladder is a spiritual ladder towards a higher planes in perspective to the manifested Universe. It is a ladder in which Manifested matter becomes closer to Spirit. It is also a Ladder towards the Great Spirit.

The staircase of the Goddess is a spiritual staircase that leads to subjective lower planes in perspective to the manifested Universe. It is a staircase in which manifested matter becomes closer to spiritual matter. It is a ladder to the Feminine aspect of the Great Spirit.

When both the ladder and the staircase are joined together we get the universal tree of Life.

A general theory of the state of Malkuth

Malkuth is known as the unmanifested physical Universe. It can also be thought of to be the physical universe when the elemental world is involved to create the unmanifested Universe. There is range of realness attached to Malkuth. This range is five-fold where matter can be either mundane or real. A real world is 5th dimensional and a mundane world is 1 dimensional. The definition of real, is having meaning. The mundane world is a world without meaning.

The dimensions of Malkuth

All physical things have at least 7 major energy centers.The reason for this has to do with the construction of the being star. We can call these energy points Chakras. The energy center have their reflection from the primordial elements of earth, water, fire, air, akasha, Light, and pure spirit.

The first three chakra points of a physical thing are Earth, Water, Fire; or dimension 1,2, and 3

On a side note, The first three chakra points of a spiritual matter thing are Air, Fire, Water; or dimension 4,3, and 2

The vibrations of the first three chakras have to do with all things physical, and achieving the highest potential physically.

Dimensions of Malkuth

1. Mundane
2. Meaning
3. Understanding
4. Purpose
5. Real

When analyzing our earth we can say that it vibrates right above the mundane at a 2nd dimensional frequency. The earth chakra of the earth will pertain to everything we can experience with our five senses. As we go up the chakra of the earth we get more and more spiritual.

1. Earth (Pure matter)
    1. pertain to everything we can experience with our five senses
2. Water
    1. Has to do with all the ideas that are generated by the earth and how everything on Earth interconnects
    2. An ocean of knowledge that flows from the higher chakras of the earth is accessible from the water Chakra
    3. The use of art gives more to the Water Chakra of the Earth
3. Fire
    1. The Fire Chakra of the Earth has to do with accumulated energy that was used to create the earth. The energy of fire is always present but hard to access. Access to the fire Chakra takes active work
    2. The ley lines of energy that connects everything on earth is present in the fire chakra of the earth
    3. A multiversal continuum will be able to be reached if one is able to access the fire chakra of the earth
4. Air
    1. The vibrations of the air chakra of the earth allows for a divine perspective of the earth vibrating through this chakra. The Air chakra is where the multiversal continuum is centered upon
5. Akasha
    1. The vibrations of origin are present in this Chakra. Through this Chakra, anything can be known about the earth chakra
6. Light
    1. This Chakra vibrates above all physical things. From this Chakra we can see the progress of physical matter as well as access to higher forms of matter

7. Pure spirit
    1. This chakra exists outside of physical things. From this chakra anything can be possible with physical matter

The two ways of Knowing

Knowing and understanding the physical and Spiritual universe can be done in two general ways; The way of Fire or the Way of water. Both ways are based on perspective and needs.

The fire way of knowing is of objective analysis using science and anything outside of ourselves. It is useful for objective understanding. It is also the Harder of the two warts

The Water way of knowing is subjective analysis based on systematic reflection towards truth . This is the Way of magic and dreams.

Kriya and Karma

Two spiritual forces that govern objects and beings in Malkuth are Kriya and Karma. Karma by definition is every cause has an effect. Karma is the spiritual Law of Cause and effect. Kriya however is action. It is the Law of action. Karma works against Kriya. A large amount of Kriya can stop the effect of the Karma. God's Ladder is governed by Karma, while the staircase of the Goddess generates Kriya. Karma is the domain of the Father's Universe, while Kriya is the Domain of the Goddess's universe.

The human as magi

Magi is any being imbued with magical energy. Magical energy will be defined as energy that is akashic; that is source energy. A manu will be defined as a being that has the right balance of the four elements that the akashic element is present. All humans are manu, but not all humans are magi. Magi are beings in which the Akashic element is highly present. A magi being is in a higher position than that of a god and that of an elemental being because of its existence in the material world. As such gods and elemental beings become Manu to become magi.

The five essential yogas of a magi and their medium

The path of the magi, is a spiritual path for manu beings with the goal of allowing divine source energy to flow in such a way that to be Magi is to be Divine incarnate. The medium of the Magi is to cultivate Kriya and master Karma. This is done through five essential yogas, derived from the elements.

1. Fire-Kriya: The yoga of action and energy
   1. This yoga has to do with cultivating energy for the soul and spiritual Kriya
2. Water-Bhakti: The Yoga of devotion
   1. This Yoga has to do with developing magnetic force for the soul towards the divine or a particular object
3. Air- Jnana: The Yoga of Wisdom
   1. This yoga has to do with cultivating inner knowledge and wisdom of the soul
4. Earth-Karma: The Yoga of work
   1. This Yoga has to do with mastering Karma through the soul's work
5. Akasha- Tantra: The Yoga of Magic
   1. This yoga has to do with the creative aspect of the soul using akashic energy

These five yogas are branches of the Magi. When practiced it gives the Magi the powers of the elements and a path towards strengthening the soul eternally. The ends of these five essential yogas are the divinity of the spirit-soul.

Royalty and A vessel : A crown as the perfect vessel

When a spirit becomes a form consisting of five elements, it naturally develops a kind of royalty over the elements in their pure form. As such, a manu form is a royal form in Malkuth, however only by the definition of it being a form that has balanced elements that allow Akasha to be present. The Magi views its manu form as a vessel to strengthen its royalty. This energy of royalty is increased by the divinity developed through the five essential yogas.

A Vessel

A vessel is seen as any form that a magi uses to increase its Royalty, Most prevalent being the manu form of a human. However there are vessel forms of magi all over nature.

A Crown

A crown is a perfect vessel defined by its immortality in Malkuth. A crown is the goal of every Magi, as it allows for eternal growth within the physical world of Malkuth. A genuine Magi has a crown with 9 sheaths. Such a Magi can be considered a God.

The Lord and the Shadow of Malkuth: Its many forms, elemental and beyond

It is through the light and energy of the Lord of the Physical universe that Malkuth that we know of it was created. As being situated in Malkuth, we can only begin to understand Malkuth by working with its shadow, as we are the sources of light for the shadow. It is within the shadows of Malkuth that we gain power and knowledge. The closest shadow of Malkuth is the elemental world. But there are worlds beyond this that have meaning when connected to Malkuth.

A pursuit towards a downwards Shadow spirituality in finding divinity

As such Magi spirituality is a spirituality that looks towards the shadow of Malkuth in order to prepare for an ascent upwards towards the Great Spirit. Hence the name downwards and Upwards.

The wheel of The Magi

* All a matter of perspective

Earth: At the center

Fire: At the bottom

Water: At the top

Air: to the east or west: Air takes the form of mineral

Akasha: to the east or west: Akasha takes the form of nature

11

The medicine wheel

12

Story Mechanics and its extension into MetaMath: The seers map, tool, and practice

1. The story mechanics
    1. Linguistics as source energy
        1. The order of languages
    2. The Sage Path
    3. The names of things : F(A)W=E
    4. The 12 dimensions
        1. Derivation
        2. Linear through God's Ladder
        3. Circular through the Genie circle
    5. The six directions
    6. The poetic metaphor : Fool's poetics
    7. The tool (Key 5)
        1. The Quadrivium

            1. Logic
            2. Grammar
            3. Rhetoric
            4. Magic
                1. The form of Arithmetic
                2. The form of Music
                3. The form of Symbology: Ritual and Dreams
        2. The Octavium
            1. Philosophy
            2. Mathematics
            3. Mythology
            4. Kabbalah
            5. Physics
            6. Geometry
            7. Alchemy
            8. Astronomy
    8. The Elemental vowel sounds and sound mapping
    9. Magical Ontology
    10. The Mudric Language
    11. The Steps to magical formulas
    12. Probability and Possibility: The language of the Meta-math of story mechanics
    13. Of dreams, the 4th, and the astral plane : The actualization of MetaMath
    14. The Goal: Access to the otherworld: The matrices of the tree
2. Four main focus of seership
    1. Dreamery: The ability to dream and explore the Astral
    2. Alchemy: The ability to understand and manipulate physical matter

    3. Luck and Divination: The ability to be aware of and understand probability and Change
    4. Music: The ability to manipulate and generate sound energy
3. The first 9 tarot cards as a guide to magical growth:An Ascension code

13

Linguistics as source energy

1. Linguistics as source energy
   1. Language is the main tool of the seer and the magician. It can be a representation of source energy.
      1. Aleph: Silence
      2. Beth: The word
      3. Gimel: Idea
      4. Daleth: Map
   2. To speak and to write are mystical manifestations of spirit. The study of linguistics and language is a further study in spirit. Different languages can be thought of as being different access to source energy.
   3. The study of language in the four forms is fundamental to story mechanics. There can be taught of to be four main forms of language
      1. Aleph: A language that is a mirror image to spirit: Spirit like. Zeroth ordered
         1. Everything has a language if you listen

    closely. This is the language of the universe and of particular things that cannot be spoken. If you understand the Aleph language of a thing you gain a certain understanding and control over it

2. Beth: A language that goes towards spirit: towards spirit : first order
    1. Any language that aims to describe spirit. Music can be considered a beth language. As well as different forms of art.
    2. The mudric language is a beth language.
3. Gimel: A language that goes toward other: For communication : Second order
    1. Any language that aims to communicate. All spoken languages are gimel languages
4. Daleth: A language that is towards matter: Towards matter. Third order language
    1. Any language that is created to describe matter, manipulate it, as well take order in it
    2. Mathematics is an example of a Daleth language
    3. Daleth languages are bridges to different sciences and magic

14

The sage path

The Sage path

The Wisdom of the Universe and knowledge of the six paths is found and represented by the Akashic principle. This principle is found in six defined limits

1. The Limits
    1. The Aksashic principle of the self: Subject
    2. The Akashic principle of the other:Object
    3. The Akashic principle of two spatial/temporal limits
        1. Beginning
        2. End
    4. The Akashic principle of two metaphysical worlds
        1. Upperworld
        2. Underworld
    5. The limits all connect to form a center of existence that is in the present moment and have foundations that are the six limits. We can call this center , a being or a spirit.

2. The Sage path
    1. The sage path is a path to wisdom in the universe, hidden in the soul of the Universe for those who dare to find it
3. There are three foundational representations or Keys
    1. Name
    2. Voice
    3. Home

    If one has these three things, it is a being that exists, can be communicated with, and a being that can act and grow
4. The doors

    Each Key opens two doors
    1. Name Key
        1. Your name is your identity. It is your spiritual identity. It can be considered the name given to you by God. The process of self-actualization is finding this name
        2. The name key opens to doors or paths
            1. The Path of magic
            2. The Yogic path
        3. The name key's fundamental skill is Wishing
            1. Wishing is knowledge of manifesting an unmanifested idea.
    2. Voice Key
        1. Your voice is an expression of your spirit. In order to utilize your voice you must learn.
        2. The Voice Key opens two paths
            1. The path of naming or path of Learning
            2. The Path of Art
        3. The Voice key fundamental skill is Divination
            1. Divination is knowledge and practice of obtaining knowledge of the six limits

3. Home Key
    1. Your home is your place and origins in the Universe. It is the Birth place of your Spirit . A home can exist in the six limits, Metaphysical and Spatial/Temporal
    2. The Home Key opens two doors or paths
        1. The path of Dimensions or Path of Maps
        2. The Path of Space/Time or Path of Limits
    3. The Home key fundamental skill is Dreaming
        1. Dreaming is knowledge and practice of creating and utilizing symbols to create portals, travel through them and accomplishing certain tasks

5. The symbol of Spirit and the seventh path
    1. Each path is structured dimensionally and Elementally. The Elements give the path a sense of direction and value, while the dimensions give meaning metaphysically. The 7th path, the path of balance and flow, maintains and strengthen the other six
    2. A dimension is defined as a density of existence
    3. An element is defined as a direction of existence.
6. There are two steps to path work
    1. The Theoretical stage which is infinite
    2. The practical stage which is grounded in apparent reality

15

The sage path

1. Naming Path

Element	Fire	Water	Air	Earth
Dimension	Number	Word	Harmony	Object
1	Quantity	Quality	Order	Substance
2	Analysis	Logos	Balance	Means/ Ends
3	Physics	Shadow	Eternal	Parts/ Whole
4	Light	Vibration	Virtue	Perception

2. Art Path

Element	Fire	Water	Air	Earth
Dimension	Creation	Absorption	Technology	Manifesting
1	Poetics	Energy/ Being	Code	The word
2	Design	Dreaming	Software	Time
3	Sculpture	Space	Hardware	Space
4	Music	Relation/ Time	Intelligence	Atom

3. Magic Path (Tantra)

Element	Fire	Water	Air	Earth
Dimension	Internal	Communication	Correspondence	Creation
1	Wish	Shapeshifting	Connect	Meditate
2	Imagination	Temporal travel	Attract	Work
3	Energy	Spatial Travel	Bond	Ritual
4	Dream	Universal Travel	Develop	Magic

4. Yoga Path

Element	Fire	Water	Air	Earth

Dimension	The Limbs	The Play	The Dance	The strength
1:	Asana	Pleasure	Flow	Being
2:	Mudra	Happiness	Balance	Elemental
3:	Meditation	Light	Chaos	Vessel
4:	Ashe/ Prana	Immortality	Order	Spirit

5. Maps
    1. An Objective Map that aims to explain a concept symbolically and its location in Space/ Time as well as dimensionally. The proper term being Sigil
6. Limits
    1. An abstract name is given to that concept with the intention of holding the essence of that name and concept. It is the highest limit. The proper term being sigil

16

16 parts of Naming

The Framework's Framework or 16 Parts of Naming or The shape of a thing

1. Elemental Equation of a framework
2. A Framework and its purpose
    1. The 16 parts of naming
3. The Equation
    1. Quantity
    2. Quality
    3. Order
    4. Substance
4. Thought and reasoning
    1. Analysis
    2. Logos
    3. Balance
    4. Means/Ends
5. Action

    1. Physics
    2. Shadow
    3. Eternal
    4. Part/Whole
6. Inspiration
    1. Light
    2. Vibration
    3. Virtue
    4. Perception
7. Example
8. Developing the Shape of an Art or Object
9. Mind Palace

17

16 parts of naming

A Framework is a mental representation of an idea, plan, concept. It combines Quantity + Quality into an ordered system in order to create something of substance. The equation of a framework is F(A)W=E.The fire element represents the quantitative part "(F)" and the Air element represents the functional part "()" of the equation that shows how Fire interacts with Water which is the qualitative part "(W)".The Result of these interactions will be Earth represented by (E).For now we will define an idea, plan, concept,thing as the substance created through the interaction of essence elementally and in different dimensions.

• The purpose of this Framework is to serve as an example of how a framework should be.It is my mentality to have a framework, so any endeavor that we do will have a framework.

In the practical sense There are 8 parts of a Framework.But in a theoretical sense there are 16 parts all represented by the complete naming path.The first four practical parts correlate to the second dimension and the last four Practical parts correlates to the third dimension.The reasoning in the practical parts is that any idea has to be formed in the second dimension before it can be completed in the third. This idea needs a certain kind of essence to form which is represented by Quantity, Quality,Order, and Substance. This essence is represented by the equation, so it is already accounted for. The fourth dimensional parts would the oscillating part of an idea, the part that changes, that moves, that develops. The fourth dimensional parts would be done after the practical part of the framework and the equation of the framework is developed.Depending on what the Four dimensional part of the framework is, it can alter some parts of the structure of the framework

The First Four Practical Part represented by the second dimension is Called Thought and Reason. The Second Four Practical Parts Represented by the third dimension is Action. The Four Parts represented by the first dimension is called equation. The fouth diminesional part are called inspiration.

In summary a framework is the mental representation of an idea.All ideas have an essence represented by the Akasha. An idea is the substance created through the interaction of essence both elementally and in different dimensions. The 16 parts of naming stems from the fact that the naming path has 16 names represented horizontally by the elements and vertically by the dimension.

The elements involved in constructing a framework is mostly Fire and Earth. Fire representing Schema (Theory) and Earth representing Architecture (Practicality of manifesting in all dimensions). Dimensionally speaking, the essential idea would best represented in the first dimension in an equation.The idea is then articulated in the second dimension as thought and reason. The idea is then manifested by accounting for its representation in the 3rd dimension.And in the process of manifestation a four dimensional understanding of the Architecture develops. So A frame work will have A Schema and Architecture, 4 representations

Equation of Framework

The equation of a framework has four components. The Quantity, Quality, Order, and Substance.

Quantity-This is a numerical format that assigns a number and level to a Quality.

Quality- This is metaphor and definition of a specific part of an idea attached to a number

Order- This is how the Quantity and Quality connects and the various functions that plays a role in their connection.

Substance- This is how Quantity, Quality, and Order come together to form a picture, idea, thing

Thought and Reasoning

The Thought and Reasoning of a framework has four components. The Analysis, Logos, Balance, Means/Ends.

Analysis- This is the contemplation aspect where you look at the idea and describe what is as quantifiable as possible. This part could use graphs. More equations. Anything that touches on the idea. You can imagine it being like you mentally feeling the idea with mental hands

Logos- This is the perfection of the idea, usually described in words where the words are absolute and true.The goal of a physical representation of the framework is to have it be as close to the Logos as possible.

Balance-The balance is the feasibility of the idea as it goes into physical manifestation.It accounts for the ability of the essence of the idea being able to be manifested.

Means/Ends- These are the steps, procedure, sequence of an Idea. The end would be completion, the means would be step to completion

Action

There are four components to Action. They are The Physics, Shadow, Eternal, and Part/Whole

Physics- This is the quantifiable aspect needed for the idea. For example the time, work, energy need for that idea.

Shadow- This is the actual physicality of the idea accounting for the hurdles that stop it from being the Logos

Eternal- This is the aspect of the idea that is durable throughout time. If you were to break it down, this is what would remain. This is the Gist.

Part/Whole- The part will be all the pieces that hold the idea together, the whole would be the idea itself.

Inspiration

Inspiration represents the four-dimensional part of the framework. It has to to with the motion of the idea and the evolution of it. Their are four components to Inspiration

Light- This aspect of Inspiration has to do with clarity of an Idea. As an idea evolves or is acted upon, different parts of its framework might change.Light is the ability to identify thes changes. Your ability to shine light on an idea,is your ability to precisely pick it apart and put it back together again

Vibration- This aspect of Inspiration has to do with the impact of the idea, the effect it can have, and traces the cause to that effect.

Virtue- Virtue is the representation of all the concepts, attitudes, that hold the idea together, and sparks its growth.

Perception- The perception of an Idea is how it interacts with the world around it. For example some ideas are physical, some are mental/ not so tangible.

The Framework equation as an example

The "F"and "E" part of the equation come together to form the core of the framework.The idea behind this is that fire is expansion from source (Akasha), an idea has fire to it. Earth is creation and thus all elements are represented in it. The "()" and "W" represent a kind of malleable shell of an idea in which () is both a mediator and function that attaches discovered key concepts (W) to the core. In no way is (F) greater or lesser than (W), they complement each other. (W) is magnetic in the sense that it attaches to the core and compresses it into manifestation

The quantitative parts are separated by levels each with individual qualities attached to a number.

The first level are called Pillars/Principles which are fundamental and is the ground to the rest of the framework,The Principles consider the four elements (Though we have notions of higher element but that is beyond our comprehension as of the moment, the higher dimensions consider that one is an Avatar and has the ability to measure and feel those higher dimensions). The first level only considers Fire and earth as two opposing ends that complement each other Well formed belief and Manifestation of that belief. The second level are called structures and are represented by the 4 dimensions of creation. The third level are the 16 names of the idea concept, when fully mapped out the path to understanding and realization is opened.

The fourth level exists as the shell. It is the level of representations. The best way to explain representations are using body parts. They are the fingers to hands. Representations are elementally defined and can be numerous. Representations are discovered key concepts that help the idea function. In this fourth level we have () which is how these representations connect to the core.

Core

- First level: 2 Principles: Schema and Architecture
- Second Level: 4 Structures :Thought and Reasoning,Action, Inspiration, Equation
- Third level: 16 names
- Shell
- Fourth Level: () Representations

Developing the Shape of an Art or Object

In order to find the general shape of a thing we follow this process

1. Look for representations of the Art or Object and assign an element to them

2. Minimize the representations so that you have representations that account for all the 5 elements of that Art.

3. Develop the Four Pillars or (Equation, Thought-reasoning, Action, Inspiration)

a. What is the Equation with its four parts?

b. What is the Thought-Reasoning with its four parts

c. What is the Action with its four parts

d. What is the Inspiration with its four parts

4. What is the F(A)W=E, draw a symbol that best represents your understanding of this art or Object

IT is my theory that everything that is physical and Astral can be understood using the 16 parts of naming. The important part of this process is that it takes into consideration representations which are limitless and tries to constrain that so we can understand a particular thing

Mind Palace

A mind palace is a home for the name and shape of a thing.

The symbol

⍰

Parts of a mind palace

There are six sides off the cube. Four sides of the cube represents the elements and their meaning in obtaining a magical memory.

Right-Fire: Represents the memory equation

LTM+STM= MTM

Left-Water:: Represents the Artistic and creative absorption of knowledge as it is put into the equation

Back-Air: Represents the name and shape of information as it turned into a journey of completion

Front -Earth: Represent the application and existence of

information in the plane that it occupies. The ends to the means or the end of the journey.

Point in middle- Akasha: Represents the abillity to sense the knowledge at all times. In order to recreate things as part of yourself, you have to be able to sense it with your spirit given the faculties of your sense. Every knowledge you try to make a part of you, you have to see and feel it. First you sense it, then you expand it, then you give it energy.

Floor- Usefulness: The floor represents the usefulness of knowledge to you. If a piece of knowledge is not used or appreciated, then it is easier for it to not vibrate with you. The usefulness is something that keeps the cube together

Cover:Repetition/Autosuggestion: In order to seal the info inside of you after you build its structure, you have to repeat it over and over until it is in your mind and vibrates with you forever.

The mind palace poem

I use the mind palace and it's cube structure to develop a magical memory

Fire is the equation of knowledge
Water is the creative absorption of knowledge
Air is the process of knowledge
Earth is the Application of knowledge
Akasha is feeling of knowledge
The floor of knowledge is its usefulness
Repetition is merging with knowledge

18

Elemental dimensions

Key 1- Elemental dimensions

1. The Sigil
2. Key 1 is a representation of Being in the form of Elements and Dimensions. This provides a quality to being that can be manipulated. Mastery of the elements is crucial to magic and growth.
3. The Considerations
    1. The little elements
        1. The little elements are elements that are fundamental to existence and are inherent in all things. They are the building blocks of magic and understanding the universe. They are
            1. Fire
            2. Water
            3. Air
            4. Earth

    5. Akasha (source)
2. The big elements
    1. The big elements are higher forms of the little elements and they are also building blocks of existence and are inherent in all things. They are keys to higher forms of magic. They are
        1. Time-Fire
        2. Space-Water
        3. The Word-Air
        4. The Atom- Earth
        5. God-Akasha
3. The two forms
    1. There are two forms of Elemental being. The Balanced form is represented by the Being star. The flowing form is represented by the Medicine Wheel
        1. The Being star
        2. The Medicine Wheel
4. Dimensions of the elements
    1. On the being Star
    2. On the Medicine wheel

19

The Lords circle

The Lord's circle

1. Being star
    1. Two representation
        1. three dimensional (Elemental)
        2. Four dimensional (Story Mechanical)
2. Genie circle
    1. Derivation
    2. Goal
3. The Sigils

The Being Mind and The Genie Mind

54

- Recall that the being star is rigid representation of the dimensions where both time and space are fixed. Recall that the being star has a four-dimensional equivalent where everything is static, time and space are either/or (Refer to page 34). These two stars have a wealth of info and are powerful tools of understanding.

- 1. The Being ~~mind~~ star has two representations
  1. The 3-dimensional representation
  2. The four-dimensional representation (String Mechanics)

- M. The Being star is projection of Being. Being is your own personal universe in which you can travel or create it. A ~~[illegible]~~ [illegible] balanced Being is centered in the [illegible] of the soul, the [illegible]

The Being Stars allows us to travel across dimensions with our Being. No place is out of reach. The past, the future, the upper world, as the underworld, as well as self [illegible] other are within reach. The [illegible] of The Being Mind is to be anything you want.

2. The Genie ~~mind~~ circle is about cycling. It is also a representation of time. While the Being Star can be said to be a representation of space, the Genie circle can be said to be a representation of time. The key to deriving the genie mind is to (1) Rotate Being Star so that the vertical dimensions are now going horizontally

7 → 1

* The reason we do this is so that we can combine it with its [illegible] equivalents.

(2) Combine the 3 dimensional Being Star with the four-dimensional Being Star

1, 7 + 12, 6

* [illegible] in [illegible] with 12 to be on top and 6 to be on the bottom.

53

The Genie Circle

or

The Lords Circle

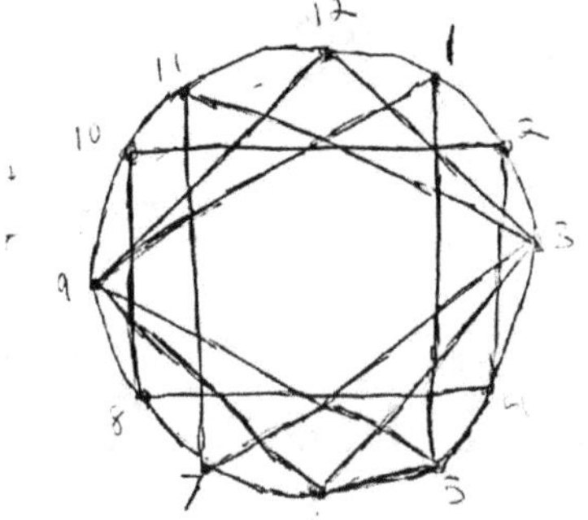

- Within this map is the key of Time and the universe

- It is also a representation of how a spirit can exist in the 3-[illegible] world with all its powers

20

Fool's Poetics: A Theory

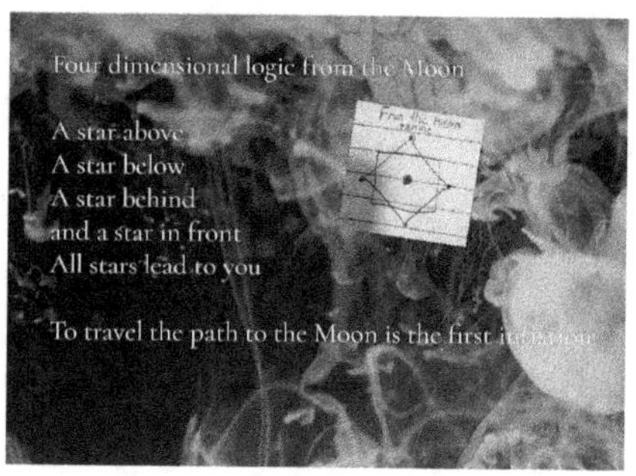

A Journey to Mastery in writing: A poet searching for The theory of everything

level 1: Copying :Novice

The process of replicating the means and end of a particular art or skill in order to produce an end just like it.

Level 2: Comparing: Apprentice

The realization of different ways of reaching a creative end through the process of comparing different ways of doing the same thing

Level 3: Compiling: Journeyman

Actively collecting ways of doing things differently. The accumulation of different tips and tricks.

Level 4: Computing :Mastery

Gaining the ability to see the bigger picture and connect everything you learned with reasonable applications.

Level 5:Coordination: Expert

Gaining the ability to coordinate and refine different tips to achieve specific objectives.

Level 6: Creating: God tier

Gaining the ability to synthesize and create entirely new ways of doing things from seemingly unrelated concepts. The Fundamentals of an Art of becomes apparent and are wielded as a tool.

The concept of poetry highlights the curse of language. There was a point in time when there was no need for language, where objective reality was not constrained by subjective words. I view poetry or any form of narrative expression as a gift to soothe the curse of subjective experience. It is a sort of telepathy in which the goal is to take my objective thoughts/ideas and transfer it on to paper or any related medium in hopes that as someone reads it,they will get to experience my thoughts/ideas as close as possible to its original form. Language as our main form of communication and descriptive tool is limited in describing experience, and the narrative craft soothes the pain of the handicap. The only way to get closer to transferring objective experience of ideas, thoughts, and objects is to become better at the craft in such a way that the finishing piece strikes the reader as a wording of his own highest thoughts.

Poetry helps capture real things. Real things wither away with time as the poetry that captures it stands the test of time. This brings the realization that while language is a curse far away from objective reality, it is also a gift when packaged into good poetry and narrative.

While objective experiences are constantly fleeting, good poetry and prose have the power to capture collages of the real as the real submits to time and change. The poet is a seer, and a good poet has the power to reach the unknown through poetry.

What is the purity of thought and ideas? Where do our ideas and thoughts come from? Where is the home of the world hidden(or created) between the words? These are the questions a poet has the ability to express and explore in their writing. When I say "world between words", I mean a location in time, space, how and why. A location that is beyond but so intricately linked to the "now and here."

I think it is time to view art for what it is. The artist is not the creator of art in the sense that he did not bring it into existence like it was never previously existing somewhere. In the physical world, it may seem as if the artist is the source of his creation. But the artist deep down knows that he is nothing but a medium. A great sadness comes across the artist, for as a medium he is limited in his efforts of bringing his inspiration (the Art) from its home without butchering it. This he knows is a great responsibility. The Art or the thing that lives somewhere else is a pure thing greater than what is put on to paper or canvas. Knowing this, the artist realizes that in order to bring this thing into this world as close to its pure form, he has to become a better medium. To do this he must become pure himself, he must hone his craft, hone his mind so that he can translate this pure thing to man in the "now and here".This is the intimate philosophy that I view the work of writing or any creation for that matter.

There are two ways one can write poetically. The first way is what I call the spirit of story. In this way, a writer or storyteller prepares themself a concept and simply writes off of that concept with no clear direction or end goal. This way of writing is how I was first introduced to the magic of storytelling.The writer can write what they see in their mind's eye.The downside of this way is that the final product can be bizarre with no clear indication of end and consideration of craft elements. The upside is that it can be very fun, and allows the writer to experience what they write. This first way is like digging for gold.

The second way of writing is what I call the mechanics of story. Or the less fun term "plotting." This way of writing is how a writer becomes a better storyteller because they take an active role in being a medium for the spirit of story. There are different plot structures available to mimic. The most famous being the hero's journey where a character leaves a place of comfort to go to a place of discomfort, and returns to his place of comfort having changed in some way.

Poetics as an Object

The object in study in Poetics is essence in the third dimension. The third dimension is physical reality as it takes the medium of words. Poetics has the most flexibility of the Arts in describing essence because it exists near the Logos/Spirit realm. However as an Art, it is only a shadow of the physical realm.

The substance of poetry is immaterial in Nature. The Logos is absolute in such a way that whatever it says exists. Man's perception of the Logos is absolute in such a way that its environment has a manifestation outside of the physical realm, and exist in a state of possibility. The mind of man is in reality trying to mimic the logos, for the logos is the mind of God, the infinite and all powerful. So as such, man aims to mimic the Logos, which is perfect. It is this concept of absorbing and mimicking the Logos, that is the substance of poetry.

God is an architect, and the world his art. Poetics honors this and aims to mimic the Art of God. We must become an architect like God and learn from God. The Poet takes pleasure in capturing the Logos in the third dimension. The means is of deep meditation and observation of the Logos In order to do that we must observe the Logo's shadow and look for qualities at the heart of it. The end of poetics is a depiction of the Eternal Logos, so that it can be shared and adored.

Poetics as a Door

The finished piece of Poetics is only finished in the Physical realm, which is a shadow of the Logos. The perfect poem is that of a door into an infinite realm.So a finished piece is a door.

Parts of the Door

The fundamental parts of the door is that of Space which consists of **line, stanza,** and **time** in the form of length. These I believe exist before the words themselves. The words just fill up the space of these. We can also delve into the sound of the words and their vibrations but that is a treatise of its own

1.Words

We can do an entire treatise of words if given the chance because words are an object themselves, and they too have purposes and ends. The sound and vibration of the words are fundamental in nature and essential to music.

Narration:Opening the Door and Entering The Realm

Narration is an opening of the door to show the realm that the door of poetry guards. It is like a brief tour or taste of the realm. The more narration develops the less important the parts of the parts of the door becomes because narration shows something more than the door. Narration aims to propel poetry into the fourth dimension of perception and it aims to give a sense of wholeness to the realm.

The goal of narration is to bring poetics to life so it is given tremendous responsibility. The substance of Narration is a three-fold frame that consists of Epic, Comedy, and Tragedy. These three frames aim at helping narration mimic life. These three frames can also be considered basic genres. The center of these three frames are characters and what they want and their ways of getting what they want.

1. Epic: The pursuit of something that is unknown, where only the surface can be seen. As the narration expands so do the things that are able to be seen. The character grow as well as the world.

2. Tragedy: The limitations of actions by certain agents and its effect on the entire world, no matter how small or large. It is quantifiable in the change in the world and its characters.
3. Comedy: The chaos of the world where there is a battle of expectations vs what actually happens. It also consists of peculiar things that diverge from the norm. It is hard to define comedy as it is subjective in nature.

The Layers of Narration

There are six parts of Narration

1. Narrator/ Perspective: The most intimate part of narration is perspective and the narrator. There are many types that suit different needs but it must be consistent with the laws of aesthetics.
2. Plot: The structure of events as it is told by the narrator. The goal of the plot is holding the substance and narration together. Its goal is to transfer the substance of a work throughout the whole of the story. Plot has many layers and variations.
3. Setting: The place that the narration stands on. It also has the role of supporting the entire narrative. Setting includes the entire environment a piece is written in.
4. Characters: Characters are the moving parts of the narratives. As the substance of narrative grows so do the characters. They also move the substance along the plot and throughout the setting
5. Reasoning: Reasoning is a mathematical aspect of narrative. It is the logical aspect of a story in which events have rational moments consistent with the norms established. A writer must have the ability to say what is implicit in a situation and appropriate to it. A writer must also be able to show what kind of thing would happen in accordance to probability and necessity.

6. Song: Song is the artistic element of Narrative and is most important for chiseling the narrative, least important for developing Aspects of song are word diction and beauty of narration. Song is the aspect that is developed with editing and to create music, this is the level of narrative that one has to expand upon.

21

Magical ontology

Magical Ontology or Kamarian Logic

=

1. Magical ontology will be considered the basis for magical reasoning. The symbol of Magical Ontology is the four dimensional being star being equal to the three-dimensional being star. What this means is that the imagination equals reality. If you limit what is possible you limit your reality. If you expand your Imagination to include things that are impossible, you expand your reality.
2. The top bar if the = sign can be thought to be the four dimensional being star which is also known as the story star as it allows for anything to be possible because it acknowledge the greatness of the fourth dimension, and its ability to change the third dimension. This bar also represent Dreams
3. The bottom bar represents the physicality of that dream.

It represents the energy and path required for such a four-dimensional logic to exist in the three-dimensional world. This logic can be taken across all dimensions. It can also thought of backwards in that a lower dimension has the potential to move something in the higher dimension but that change is smaller because of the nature of dimensions

4. The absolute meaning of the symbol is thc supremacy of a higher dimension over a lower one in regards to control
5. The space inbetween is the energy and path to manifestation

22

Magical Worlds

The Magical Worlds

Creation exists in five magical worlds. So a magical act mimics creation in a smaller sense. These magical worlds are the foundation for the five part magical act. The five dimensional being star represents each world of a magical act.These worlds are

1. The Akashic world (8th and 0th dimension)
    1. The world of Akasha ; This world is the world of source. Creation started from one point, one source. Akasha is the source of all things, all knowledge, abilities, and worlds. It is the source of magic
2. The Archetypal world (7th and 1st dimension)
    1. The world of all ideas in its purest form, its purest will.
3. The Creative world (6th and 2nd dimension)
    1. This world is variations of that pure will
4. The formative world (5th and 3rd dimension)
    1. This world is the patterns and process. It is the forces

behind the veil of physical things . It is the world of science. The world of Art, the world of magic. It is the spirit world

5. The Material world
   1. This is the world of actual forms and is the accumulation of and shadow of the previous worlds

23

Magical Energy

Magical energy

1. Energy in general comes in many forms as we have come to learn. There is electricity, chemical, Kinetic, thermal. Magical energy however is different from regular energy only in the sense that it has an intent-will attached to it
2. If we recall Kamarian logic = ,in which the upper bar represents the four-dimensional possibility being star, and the lower bar being the three-dimensional world. Another analogy is that the top bar is the limitless spirit world and the lower bar being the three-dimensional world. Another Analogy is that the top bar is the limitless spirit world and the lower bar being the rigid physical world. The upper bar has power over the lower bar when one solves the riddle of what connects the two.
3. What connects the two is energy and direction of that energy. When spirit is focused it can move the dimension below it.
4. Types of energy in a magical sens

1. All energy can be reduced to being beingness and then consciousness then a kind of physical energy. That is, there is a consciousness behind heat, behind kinetic energy
    1. 1st dimension: Beingness
    2. 2nd dimension: Consciousness
    3. 3rd dimension: Kinetic
    4. 4th dimension: Vibrational (electro-magnetic)
    5. 5th dimension: Sound
    6. 6th dimension: Light
    7. 7th dimension: Spiritual
    8. 8th dimension: Akasha

24

Mudric Language

The Mudric Language

The Mudric Language is a language of understanding a magical act, as well as recreating it. It is a system in which magic is a science that can be tracked and built on. Magic works by connecting the individual spirit to to the Universal spirit. The mudric language is a language is a generation of magic power that is aided by key 0-2

1. The Magical Worlds
    1. The Five magical Sheaths or Koshas
        1. The heart (Akasha)
            1. Through this Kosha magic can be done by will. The Heart is the imagination and the source of magic.It contains the four Ideas
                1. Time
                2. Space
                3. Word
                4. Atom

2. Buddhi (Air)
    1. The Intellect and the Intuition of Magical understanding
3. Manas (Fire)
    1. The magical will power and physical understanding
4. Prana (Water)
    1. The physical energy . It is the most important energy for physical magic, as well as magical energy in general
5. Matter (Earth)
    1. The physical body of a thing and its atomic compositions

2. The basis of the mudric language is its two symbolic forms known as the magical worlds. These representations mimic creation and must be use together
    1. The five dimension star ◈
        1. This star represents a magical act as it moves through the five magical worlds. If the sufficient magical energy is given, the magical intention will be manifested in the physical world or in the worlds below the Akashic world
            1. Akasha
            2. Fire
            3. Water
            4. Air
            5. Earth
    2. The DONAIEU mantra
        1. The IDONAIEU mantra is a reflection of the five dimensional star but it can be chanted . Sound is used to generate magical

energy as well as concentrate the intentions of the mind. It can also be looked as a type of equation. It exists in the three magical worlds

1. O
   1. Represents the Akashic world. In this part of the mantra the magical intentions are articulated. It could be a picture, a sigil, or a sentence. Pronounced as OH
2. I(DONAIEU)
   1. Represents the Archetypal world. In this part of the mantra the will power to carry out magical actions are generated. The intentions developed is purified into its purest form and chanted
3. H-N (donaieu)
   1. In this world the mantra is chanted and the magical intention is given creative direction as to how it is carried out
4. V(donaieu)'
   1. Represents the formative world. The mantra is chanted and the specific steps, patterns and processes are represented. By now the magical intent is given form and is ready to manifest

5. H-D (donaieu)
    1. Represents the material world. The mantra is chanted so that the previous mantra energies could be manifested
2. The equations have elemental and polarity representations that adds specifically to the mantra
    1. D (↑)
        1. Represents the electric principle and the process of going into an electric state
    2. O (=)
        1. Represents the spiritual Akashic energy generated from source
    3. N(↓)
        1. Represented the magnetic principle and the process of going into the magnetic state
    4. A(-)
        1. Represents the fire element . It is the process of different things being expanded on
    5. I (+)
        1. Represents the water element / The process of differentiated things being added together
    6. E (÷)
        1. Represents the Air element. It is the process of balancing .
    7. U (x)

            1. Represents the process of creation
      3. With these representations in mind we can see how various mantras can do different things
      4. Mantras
         1. The Heart: The Akashic World: 0
            1. Odonaieu
         2. The buddhi: The Archetypal World: 1
            1. Idonaieu
         3. Manas: The creative world: 2
            1. H-ndonaieu
         4. Prana: The formative world: 3
            1. V-donaieu
         5. Matter: The material world: 4
            1. H-ddonaieu
2. Yoga-Magic Connection (Energy)
   1. In order for a magical act to happen, it needs energy that is shaped by the will. Energy is the connector for the magical structure. This energy can be generated in various ways. But the most straightforward way is to generate the energy your self, which is the ultimate goal of the practice of magic.
   2. Two types of energy production
      1. Creation: Spirit to matter
      2. Destruction: Matter to spirit
   3. Ways of Generating Magical energy
      1. Elements
      2. Mantra
      3. Music
      4. Alchemy

3. Magical Architecture
    1. The Law of Cause and Effect
    2. Kamarian logic or Magical ontology is the basis of magical reason.
    3. Magical Architecture is guided by the 16 parts of magic. This part of the mudric language designate in what way will a magic act be done. Through water magic, fire magic, air magic, earth magic, or a mixture of the four.
    4. Magic Path (Tantra)

Element	Fire	Water	Air	Earth
Dimension	Internal	Com-mun-icative	Corresp-ondence	Creation
1	Wish	Shapeshifting	Connect	Meditate
2	Imagination	Temporal travel	Attract	Work
3	Energy	Spatial Travel	Bond	Ritual
4	Dream	Universal Travel	Develop	Magic

4. The Map (Sigil)
    1. The map or sigil: An objective map that aims to explain a concept symbolically and its location in space-time as well as dimensionally.
    2. The three parts of a map
        1. Symbol
            1. Its sigil and what it is doing

   2. Location in space-time
      1. The time expectation and location
   3. Dimension
      1. What dimension the magic is operated in
5. The Limit (Totem)
   1. This encloses the magical act in such a way that it can be contained, examined, and underwood. This can be a surrounding area, a statue, a specific feeling, jewelery. The totem can be looked at the end goal of the magic; Where it is nested.
6. The World
   1. The world outside magic. This is anything independent of the magical act that can be used to examine, and improve the magical structure. It is the results of the magical structure. Every magic that is done utilizes this structure.
7. The Sigil

25

Formula and Practice

The steps to magical formulas

1. Mudric Language (theory)
2. Scroll (Theory set for practice)
3. Tome: A book about that particular magic and its implication
4. A spell: A condensed form of that magic based on the wisdom gained from practice, experience, and energy
5. An Arcanum: A genuine understanding of that type of magic in such a way that one gains mastery of that type of magic. It is a condensed form of a tome.

The Eight Magical Practices

1. The Core Meditation
    1. Formlessness
    2. Energy Absorption
    3. Imagination

    4. The Secret
2. Dimensional Being
    1. This is essentially the practice of being in the present moment and strengthening our water being
3. Elemental Harmony
    1. This is essentially making sure that our being is harmonized elementally. That is it is centered in the fourth dimension
4. Imagination and Energy
    1. This is the process of concentrating and strengthening our imagination so that we get in touch with the four elements as well as develop a stronger imagination
5. Projection of Spirit and Void
    1. This is the practice of being able to project our spirit as well as entering the void
6. Wishing
    1. This is the practice in which we have a particular wish that we work to make a reality
7. Divination

   This is where we use maps to describe things and gain knowledge
8. Dreaming
    1. This the practice of mastering the dream gates

26

The Octavium

The Octavium (Light Magery)

1. Philosophy
    1. the study of the fundamental nature of knowledge, reality, and existence, especially when considered as an academic discipline.
2. Mythology
    1. refers to a body of stories that attempt to explain the origins and fundamental values of a given culture and the nature of the universe and humanity.
3. Alchemy
    1. any magical power or process of transmuting a common substance, usually of little value, into a substance of great value.
4. Mathematics
    1. Mathematics is the science and study of quality, structure, space, and change

5. Kabbalah
    1. This Kabbalist oral tradition contended that God is perceivable as 10 different potencies or forms of light; Also various cosmology relating to the macro and micro universe
6. Astronomy
    1. Astronomy is the study of everything in the universe beyond Earth's atmosphere
7. Geometry
    1. properties of space such as the distance, shape, size, and relative position of figures.
8. Physics
    1. the natural science of matter, involving the study of matter, its fundamental constituents, its motion and behavior through space and time, and the related entities of energy and force.

The Trivium

1. Logic
2. Grammar
3. Rhetoric

27

The First Arcanum

1. The First Arcanum
    1. The 8 basic powers and its sigil
        1. A description of the First Divine symbol
            - The first divine symbol is a diagram of spirit and its connection to source. The inner circle is objective experience. The forks and dashes represents the extension of source into subjective experience
            - The practice of your powers is defined as the movement of this consciousness point towards the center
            - Four parts
                1. Eight directions
                2. Four dimensional circle
                    1. Eight dimensions of the middle world
                3. The tridents of being (Universal)

        1. Spirit
        2. Soul
        3. Body
    4. The three layers of existence
        1. Upperworld
        2. The middle world
        3. Underworld
2. 8 powers
    - Possession
    - Dreaming
    - Light
    - Dark
    - Positive tuning (Magnetic)
    - Negative tuning (Electric)
    - Past
    - Future
3. The Meditation symbol and the three worlds
    - The Mediation Symbol is a useful symbol for mediation and Magic
        1. In the Underworld Stage you are able to feel relaxed as your consciousness travels towards ether. You do not yet feel immersed into Universal consciousness but you feel the otherness of it
        2. In the Middle world stage, the highlight of this state is that you are able to draw on etheric energy as the dimensions begin to connect. In this state you have access to more dimensional knowledge of the particular sector. In most cases, it would

be self. You can think deeply about self. You are still aware of the Physical world .This is the world in which daydreaming happens

3. In the upper world, you are no longer aware of your physical body. Instead you emerged into your energetic aspect. You are able to generate energy by drawing on Universal energy . You can think about the past and the future vividly as well as the other and self. You have access to Akasha.
4. In the etheric world, you feel a deep connection to the universe, and can begin actively traversing to other directions.

4. Degree of Control (Mathematical)
   - There is something called degree of control, which has to dow with the dimensional worlds. There are 8 degrees of control. Each increasing in difficulty after linear.
     1. Zeroth (Degree 0)
     2. Linear (Degree 1)
     3. Quadratic (Degree 2)
     4. Cubic (Degree 3)
     5. Quartic (Degree 4)
     6. Quintic (Degree 5)
     7. Sextic (Degree 6)
     8. Septic (Degree 7)
     9. Octic (Degree 8)
5. Procedures of control
   - Layer 1 (The Ideal layer)

1. Degrees 0-3
- Layer 2 (The real layer)
   1. Degree 4
- Layer 3 (The control layer)
   1. Degree 5-8

2. Mastery of Key 0
   1. Its qualification and Genesis poem

      Out of the void comes spirit with 7 chakras

      The seven chakras of spirit connects to seven chakras of some form

      The seven chakras of form connects to seven chakras of body
   2. The three selves
      - Ancestral self
      - The Manu self
      - The Elemental self
   3. Dream gates and an analysis of Dreaming
      - The Mastery of Key 0 entails mastering the seven Dream Gates. Mastery of the gates will result in a spirit being capable of many things, notably spirit travel across the three worlds
   4. The Four Hidden books : The core
      - Book 1 (Key 0)- Void
      - Book 2 (Key 1)- Imagination
      - Book 3 (Key 2)- Energy absorption
      - Book 4 (Key 3)- The Secret
3. ALA in practice: The inbetween
   1. The Dream Story sigil
   2. The four states sigil towards a quantum reality
   3. The four fundamental understanding of reality (All is ALA)

- Akasha: All is from ALA
- Water: Prepare for a return to ALA
- Fire: All is a result of ALA
- Earth: ALA is present

4. The general practice sequence
    - Awareness : Earth to Air (Realm of Self)
    - Awareness : Air to Water; Air to Fire (Realm of Dreams)
    - Awareness : Water to Akasha (Realm of the Underworld)
    - Awareness: Fire to Akasha (Realm of the Ancestors)

4. Four World Meditation
    1. Atziluth : Visualization of Key 0 and Mathematics
    2. Briah : Visualization of Key 0 and the Word
    3. Yetizirah: Visualization of Tree of Life and its many variations
    4. Assiah: Visualization of 5th dimensional space
5. The deeper Arcanum of the Magi
    1. The Gate cycle sigil
    2. Gate 0 opening
    3. Gate 1 opening
    4. Gate 2 opening or the Arcanum towards God-hood of 4 sheaths
6. The 7 part sigil: A key to actual magic
    1. Chakra theory
    2. The formula for creating a magical sigil
    3. The four main sigils
        - A sigil for Dreamery
        - A sigil for Alchemy
        - A sigil for Luck and Divination
        - A sigil for Music

28

Scrolls of Gate 1 and Gate 0

Scrolls

Scrolls of Gate 0

1. The Meditation symbol
2. The Dream self
3. The core meditation
4. The Cycle of Life and death
5. The First divine
6. The opening of Gate 0
7. The opening of Gate 1

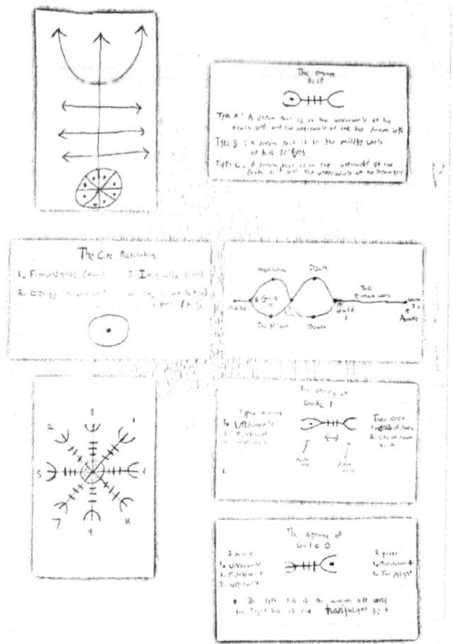

Scroll of Gate 1

1. How dreams arise
    1. Dreaming Happens in either one of the five worlds from the perspective of the manu body. The best types of dreams to have are akashic dreams as it connects both three worlds. Dreaming naturally happens in the fourth dimension
2. Dream energy
    1. The energy of dreams is sourced from the Archetypal body and the Elemental body naturally by design. The Adamanic body however have to actively seek to strengthen the dream body.
3. The names of this scroll
4. Gate 1 Sigil
5. The Dream totem
6. The World of dreams

1. Dream Journal
2. The Astral world
3. The Underworld

29

The Aura Scroll

The Aura Scroll or The Seer's scroll

1. Definition of Aura
   1. An Aura is the energy in a thing/being , and the energy emanating from the thing/being. A simplification of Aura is awareness. The Aura corresponds to the five magical world of the three of live

Eternal cycle	Dimension	Awareness level	Kabbalis-tic underst-anding	Tarot understanding
Aleph	0	Akashic Awareness	10 sefirots	The fool

Beth	1	Spiritual Awareness	The three foundational letters	Magician
Gimel	2	Soul Awareness	The seven double letters	Divinity
Daleth	3	Physical Awareness	The twelve simple letters	Crown

In Advanced studies the above is on Aura emanating from light and there is also an aura emanating from darkness, also known as shadow kabbalah. This is your personal crown in the shadow world. Your own personal sun which becomes a moon in the middle world

2. Auric energy
   1. The Aura in each world has energy correspondence according to the energy sigil

1.

Akashic Awareness	Generate	Spiritual Energy: Art
Spiritual Awareness	Destroy	Light:sound
Soul Awareness	Enhance	Electromagnetism:Vibration

Physical Awareness	Act	Consciousness:Beingness

3. Auric Magic

Fire Magic	Water Magic	Air Magic	Farth Magic
10 Sephiroth	Akashic Awareness	Generate (Aleph)	Art
Three fundamental letters	Spiritual Awareness	Destroy (Beth)	Light:sound
Seven double letters	Soul Awareness	Enhance (Gimel)	Electromagnetism
Twelve simple letters	Physical Awareness	Act (Daleth)	Consciousness: Beingness

4. The Auric Map
   1. Aleph (Vertical line)
   2. Beth (Horizontal line)
   3. Gimel (Cross +)
   4. Daleth (Pyramid)
5. The Auric totem
   1. The totem of Auras are anything that is physical or have beingness
6. The World
   1. Light
   2. Sound
   3. Sensation
   4. Smell

5. Taste

30

Shadow Kabbalah Scroll

Shadow Kabbalah Scroll (Shadow Magery)

1. The Magical worlds of Shadow Kabbalah
   1. The Manu form is an evolved form that has the potential to wield chaos and order. It is the physical form of integrated masculine and feminine divinity of the eternal father and the eternal mother. This knowledge comes from the Akashic world. The symbolic form of man in masculinity is 6 pointed star. The symbolic form of man in femininity is the five pointed pentagram. The divine man is four dimensional.
   2. Every Physical form is composed of the elements in its own hidden capacity. Man's Consciousness and elemental makeup is of Clay. That is the make up of man that allows for the potential for order and chaos is a pristine joining of the elements. This is both a gift and a shortcoming as man must work to go back to source, however

    the strengthening of the pristiness of form is gained being made of clay
  3. When one takes the path of Magic, One takes the path of mastering and understanding one's own chaos. This practice is known as Magery. The Physical Body is made up of elements. Every physical forma has a shadow sun that was used to create it. Magery is tapping into that that underworld sun to understand one's own connection to source. It is here that one draws magical energy. Science, however, is understanding the upperworld sun and drawing knowledge and energy from that source.
  4. The Underworld Sun has a symbolic story. This is the story that was used to create the Adamanic form
     1. 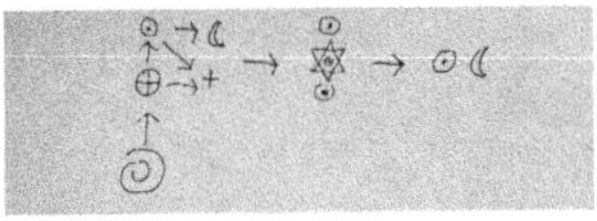
     2. This is the symbolic story of man. Its meaning will stay hidden as the symbols speak for itself. As such the Elemental beings or nature that have gain mastery over the four elements, incarnate into the clay body of man to chase their upperworld sun.
     3. This magical key is the key of assuming elemental form while in the clay form of man. This is done by drawing energy from your underworld sun. Every Physical form has a unique Underworld Sun
2. The Energy for Shadow Kabbalah
   1. The process of drawing energy from your underworld sun uses the energy sigil. The goal of the practices uses four elemental keys known as books to transfer beingness to energy to spirit in fluid fashion

3. The Architecture of Shadow Kabbalah

1.

Dimension	Fire	Water	Air	Earth
1	Magic	Lord	Domain	Underworld
2	Symbolic story	Master	Understand	Aspire
3	Underworld Sun	Power	Crown	Seek
4	form	Manu	Adamanic	Magic

4. The Sigil of Shadow Kabbalah

1. 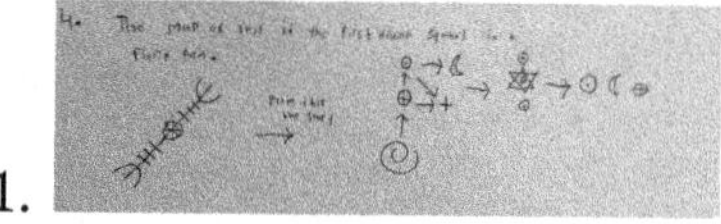

5. The totem of Shadow Kabbalah
    1. The totem for Shadow Kabbalah is the Physical form that is Clay. Also this story can be used to understand other physical forms

31

Elemental book scrolls

Elemental Books

1. Elemental Book 1: The Book of Nature
    1. The book of the wilderness
    2. Key 0
    3. Step 1
    4. This book utilizes key 0 in it's entirety, however it focuses on the underworld self as a reflection of the first divine. This meditation focuses on the Underworld self that is master and lord of form that is the clay body. This self is like the first divine in the sense that its only concern is your physical form.
2. Elemental Book 2: The Astral Mirror
    1. The Book of Imagination
    2. The book of the magician
    3. The book of the Underworld Self
    4. The Astral Mirror

5. Key 1
6. Step 2
7. This book utilizes Key 1 in its entirety to form the magical self that is in caly. From this key, the imagination becomes boundless as you draw from the lord self. Such a key is meant to make the underworld sun's connection to the body as pristine as possible. This meditation allows one to meditate on all elemental aspects of the spirit

3. Elemental Book 3 : The Book of Divinity
   1. The Book of Energy
   2. The Book of Absorbtion
   3. Key 2
   4. Step 3
      1. This book utilizes Key 2 in its entirety. This book aims at getting in touch with the primordial element of the universe as well as universal energy that is gained from tapping into such a source. These meditations are the first steps in magical power
4. Elemental book 4: The Book of Secrets
   1. The Book of Magical Actualization
   2. Step 4
   3. Key 3
      1. This book utilizes Key 3 in its entirety. This book is the book of practical magic. This book represents the self that has touched and can control the four elements . This opens the doorway to higher forms of magic. This book utilizes the magnetic and electric forces or the forces of expansion and contraction.

Elemental Book 1 : Key 0

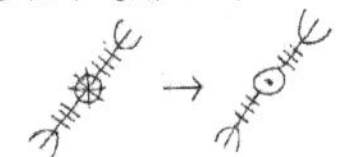

Step 1 : Void Meditation

The Book of the wilderness
or
The Book of Nature

- This Book Utilizes Key 0 in it entirety, however it Focuses on the the underworld self as a Reflection of the First divine that it. This meditation focuses on the underworld self that is Master and Lord of form that is the clay body. This self is like the first divine in the sense that its only concern is your physical form.

- This Self has a spirit, a soul, as well as a body in the underworld. It is a Lord, and you are its totem that has a spirit that is a directly sourced from the spirit of that self. Your soul was sourced from this spirit as well as your body.

- The Underworld Self is your power body
- This is the Self you meditate to.

Elemental Book 2 : Key 1

Step 2

The Astral Mirror
(imaginations)

The book of the magician
or
The Book of the underworld self

- This book utilizes Key 1 in its entirety to form the magician self that is in clay, from this Key the imaginations boundless as you draw from the Lord Self. Such a Key is Meant to Make the underworld sun's connection to the Body as pristine as possible. This Meditation allows one to meditate on all elemental aspects of the spirit.

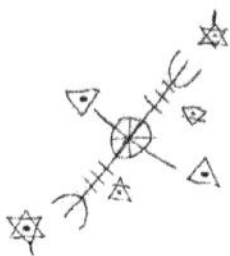

Divinity Book 3 : Key 2

Step 3

Energy Absorbtion

The Book of Divinity

- This book utilizes Key 2 in its entirety. This book uses of getting in touch with the primordial elements of the universe as well as universal energy that is gained from tapping into such source. These meditation are the first steps in magical power.

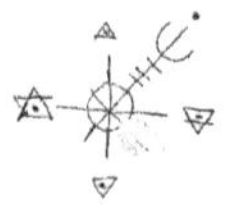

Elemental Book 4 : Key 3

Step 4

The Secret

The Book of Secrets

- This book utilize Key 3 in its entirety. This book is the book of practical magic. This book represents the Self that has touched and can control the four elements. This opens the doorway to higher forms of magic. This book utilizes the magnetic and electric forces. or the forces of expansion and contraction

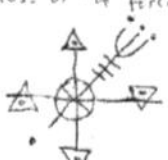

32

Spiritual Energy Scroll

Spiritual Energy Scroll

1. There are four main types of Spiritual energy
   1. The Magical energy represented by fire
   2. The Empathic energy represented by Water
   3. The Lifeforce represented by air
   4. The Form energy represent by Earth
2. Spiritual energy is based on the Astral Mirror
3. The Air element corresponds to the life force
4. The fire element corresponds to energy that can be converted to different kinds of energy using magical energy. This energy can be cultivated and transferred to the Air element
5. The Water element corresponds to the ability to feel energy
6. The earth element is the energy connection and ability to control form.
7. It is through your ability to feel that you gain mastery over the elements

8. When earth energy runs out that is when your body feels tired and when the astral form disconnects from the body. This can be nullified by converting

33

The Holy Scroll

The Holy Scroll

1. Holiness come from understanding
    1. The Tree of life
    2. Solar to lunar to earth consciousness
2. Understand come from knowing the three natures of
    1. Order
    2. Balance/flow
    3. Chaos
3. The Shadow is the teacher
4. The five holy sadhanas are
    1. Being Sadhana
    2. Pandora Sadhna
    3. Sage Path Sadhana
    4. Devata Sadhana
5. The Highest goal of a Magi is of an Emperor with a four part understanding of

  1. Power
  2. Strategy
  3. Communication
  4. Introspection
6. Magery is the perfection magic in such a way: Two main powers are
  1. Mirrors
  2. Portals

34

The Kamarian Riddle

1. The riddle
2. Oneironautics
3. Dream Cosmology
4. Griot Yoga: Or Vessel Yoga

Kamarian Riddle
Kamaria is both your origin and destination
An Avatar creates himself and so do you
Parts

1. The Moon and Beyond: 5th dimensional logic and a theory of plausibility
   1. This earth is known as the physical world. It is one of the many physical places in a plane called Malkuth. Malkuth is a plane that encompasses all of the physical world, and 4th-5th dimensional frequencies
   2. The world known as Kamaria is a theoretical Ancestral

        Planet and origin of your soul. A Kamarian Initiation is a development in Malkuth. This is important as Kamaria is a world that exists in Yesod. The fifth dimension.
    3. It is in a different space time. Hard to locate in time and space because of its 5th dimensional frequencies.
    4. Its inhabitants have jinn and genie energy and origins
2. Ancestral planets and their placement on earth
    1. What we know from Sources
    2. A list of these places
        1. Konton
        2. X
        3. X
        4. X
        5. X
3. Tales of Kamaria: A home
    1. Where do souls come from?
4. The framework of Initiation: Structure, Process, and Goal
    1. The structure of Initiation is to evolve throughout Malkuth in Preparation to Return to Kamaria
    2. Dragonfly Analogy
        1. Egg (In Kamaria)
        2. Nymph (Nymph in Malkuth)
        3. Dragonfly (In Yesod)
5. The schoolground of the Earth Zone and Locality of the Moon Zone
    1. The whole of Initiation is using Malkuth as a schoolground to Master Key 0 and Key 1 return to Kamaria in order to Master more Keys. How you do this is up to you. The blueprint of actualization is in your soul.
    2. Kamaria is an actual metaphysical place within infinity.
6. Of Genie: Origins, Classes, and powers
    1. Jinn (guixian) Of water or Fire

   2. Jinn human (Renxian) Water + Fire
   3. D'Jinn (Dixian) Master of all four elements
   4. Advanced D'Jinn (Shen Xian) Master of Dimensional nature
   5. Genie (Tianxian) Master of Time and space
7. Key 0 and 1: Incarnation,The Human form and its uses
8. The Ancestral Powers and duties
9. The Art of Dreaming: Key 0 and primary attainment of Initiation
10. Construction of the Astral Palace or Genie Lamp
    1. One of the major goals of this initiation is gaining a sense of freedom in Malkuth. One way of doing this is developing the faculty of the soul for inner dreaming. Many people are born with spiritual gifts. For example some are born with spiritual sight, some people even have psychic powers. These may be skills they developed in another life, or innate gifts of their soul nature. In this life and in death,your task is to develop the magnetic nature of your soul for inner dreaming. This is where the soul goes deeper into its own Akashic self, Existing within itself. When this becomes magnetic,it will be a gift that your soul would be able to take with it to any incarnation
11. The Test and Graduation: Becoming a Lunar Deity in Yesod (Emergence of the Dragonfly)

Oneironautics

The practice of dreaming utilizes Key 0 and Key 1 and some of Key 2. The key 0 aspect is that dreams are an essential practice of the soul and spirit. The key 1 aspect is to have more control of your dreams. The key 2 aspect is mapping the dreamworld. Oneironautics is the path that most Kamarlan avatars chose

1. Novice
    1. The novice oneironaut takes a step and uses key 0 to understand the dream world. The novice is able to remember his dreams upon will.
    2. The novice apprentice is aware of dream gates and spend most of time utilizing gate 0 (day-dreaming) and spends his time trying to open gate 1 (Lucid dreaming)
    3. The novice apprentice creates a practice or routine that allows him to lucid dream. This includes studying the tree of life and the mechanics of the astral worl
2. Apprentice
    1. The apprentice oneironaut is able to open gate 1 but still have to work to open it The opening of gate 1 gives an oneironaut the title of apprentice.
    2. While in a Lucid state the apprentice looks for a teacher, which is a deeper aspect of himself. This dream self will teach about the dream world.
    3. The apprentice oneironaut deals with his inner world and Malkuth of the tree of life.
    4. The apprentice oneironaut works on Key 1 while in the dream state as well as the waking state. This will strengthen the magical nature of his soul. This has the end goal of making opening gate 1 as easy a gate 0, and to strengthen his connection to akasha which will thus make gate 2 (dream travel) more efficient and reliable.
3. Journeyman
    1. The Journeyman oneironaut can efficiently use gate 0 and 1 constantly
    2. He uses his experience and practice of key 0 and Key 1

in application of oneironaut to work on opening gate 4 (spirit travel). This can be done in a waking state.
   3. The journeyman oneironautics is able spirit travel
   4. The journeyman oneironaut has worked on making lucid dream a principle part of his soul in such a way that this skill carries over to different incarnations
4. Master
   1. To the master oneironaut the dream world is no different that the physical world
   2. The master oneironaut can work in Yesod and travel all throughout of Malkuth
   3. The master oneironaut works on merging his dream world with the physical world.
   4. To master oneironaut reincarnation is a break in his dream world. A minor inconvenience and he uses it to strengthen connection to physical world
5. Expert
   1. An expert oneironaut can call himself a Doro. He both exists and does not exist. He can exist and not exist at will. He exists in a dream-like state that merges with malkuth's reality

Dream Cosmology

The earth is the place where all forms of life call home. It is a place where the elements intertwine. The Earth's origin, future, and mechanics is unknown to a Poet. However when one understands the nine worlds of existence, all knowledge can be found.

An understanding of cosmology will allow the dreamer to travel and understand reality in a variety of ways. In natural cosmology there are 32 vectors in which each has a locality within 7 realms

1. The Middle World (7 vectors)
2. The UnderWorld (4 vectors)
3. The Upper World (4 vectors)
4. The Objective Realm (4 vectors)
5. The subjective realm (4 vectors)
6. The Past Realm (4 vectors)
7. The future realm (4 vectors)
8. The Creator's realm (1 vector)

The Middle world is the world in which terrestrial life inhabits and in which man inhabits. It also consists of the primal and extra-terrestrial realm It consists of three different dimensions. This world consists of the present reality with 7 vectors

1. The present
2. The Past vector (veil)
3. The Future veil (veil)
4. The Beyond vector
5. The heaven veil (Veil)
6. The Objective vector (veil)
7. The subjective vector (veil)

Some vectors are called veils because an observer in the present cannot actively be in these places while in the 3rd dimension.The 3rd dimension is the present world. The Beyond veil is the 4th dimension. The heaven veil is the 5th dimension.. The past veil is in a dimension above the present and below the beyond. The past veil is a barrier/portal to the past. The future veil is a barrier/portal to the future. The Beyond veil is a portal to the Great beyond. There isn't a barrier to the Great beyond. The heaven veil is a barrier/portal to a realm above the 4th dimension. The Objective veil is a barrier/portal to objective experience of another thing outside of self. The subjective veil is a barrier/ portal to a total experience.

The Underworld is a realm below the present in which everything that makes up the present can be known on a deeper level. It consists of four vectors in two dimensions

1. The form vector
2. The past form vector (veil)
3. The future form vector (veil)
4. The Goddess's Universe vector (Veil)

The form vector is in the 2nd dimension. This vector explains the formation of everything in the present time. It is where the laws of the Universe originate. The past form is a veil/ barrier to the forms of the past. This veil connects the Underworld of the present to the Underworld of the past. The future form vector is a barrier/veil to the forms of the future. This veil connects the Underworld of the Present to the Underworld of the future realm. The Goddess's Universe Vector is a veil that connects the Middle world to a feminine reality below the Underworld. This reality is a unique reality itself with 32 vectors

The Upper world is a realm above the Great beyond in which everything that makes up the present has a higher/transcendental existence.It consists of four vectors in two dimensions

1. The Archetypal vector
2. The Past Archetype Vector (veil)
3. The future Archetype Vector(veil)
4. The Lord's Universe Vector (Veil)

The Archetypal Vector is in the 6th dimension. This vector explains the Divine hand of everything in the present time. It is where the Laws of the Universe can be manipulated and expanded upon.

The Past Archetype vector is a veil/barrier to the Archetypes of the present time in the past. This veil connects the UpperWorld of present time to the Underworld of the Lord's Universes objective reality. The future Archetype vector is a veil/barrier of Archetypal forms of the future. This veil connects the Upper World of Present time to the upper world of an individual's subjective reality.The Lord's Universe Vector is a Veil that connects the middle world to a masculine reality above the upper world. This is a unique reality itself with 32 vectors

The Reality above the Lord's realm is known as the Creator's Realm. The beings that touch this realm can be thought of to be the Creators of this present reality. It is in this realm that the Creator of this Universe inhabits.

The Objective Realm is a realm in which everyone in the Middle world shares.It is the Objective reality of the Middle World. It consists of four vectors in 2 dimensions

1. The Object-Subject Vector
2. The Object Vector
3. The Archetypal Object vector
4. The Past-Object Vector

The Subjective Realm is a realm in which a Dreamer/Observer inhabits but shares with no one. It is the subjective reality of the middle world. It consists of four vectors in 2 dimensions

1. The Subject-Object vector
2. The Object Vector
3. The Archetypal Subject Vector
4. The Future-Subject Vector

The Past Realm is a realm in which the past exists as an object. It consists of four vectors in 2 dimensions

1. The past resonance vector
2. The past-object vector
3. The past-Underworld Vector
4. The actual Past vector

The future realm is where the future exists as a subject. It consists of four vectors in 2 dimensions

1.The future resonance vector

2. The future-subject vector
3. The Future Underworld Vector

4.The actual future vector

Griot Yoga: Or Vessel Yoga

1. References
    1. Sefer Yetzirah
    2. The Initiation into Hermetics and Bardon's Spirit teachings of Key 1 2 3
2. Magical Ontology
    1. The bulk of our ontology has to do with understanding of two infinite Akasha
        1. Individual Akasha
        2. Universal Akasha
    2. The basis for magic has to do with four dimensional logic
3. Aspects
    1. The three books
        1. Text
        2. Number
        3. Communication
    2. Aura theory (experiential)(qualitative) (used to describe what is happening in magic)

1. Aura is the emanations from a thing in existence that defines it in a qualitative way
    1. The four levels of understanding
        1. Akashic awareness
            1. This is awareness and emanations of source energy within a thing.It consist of a fivc dimensional continuum. There is a Space continuum, a Time continuum, and Spiritual/ Moralistic continuum. These are concepts before the construction of Space/Time
                1. Represented by the 10 Sephiroth
                    1. Beginning (Chokmah)
                        1. Wisdom
                    2. End (Binah)
                        1. Understanding
                    3. Good (Keter)
                        1. Crown
                    4. Evil (Malkuth)
                        1. Kingdom
                    5. Up (Netzach)
                        1. Victory
                    6. Down (Hod)
                        1. Splendor
                    7. North (Geburah)
                        1. Strength

            8. South (Chesed)
                1. Love
            9. East (Tiferet)
                1. Beauty
            10. West (Yesod)
                1. Foundation
2. Spiritual awareness
    1. This is awareness of self and beingness as an extension of source. Everything has this
        1. The Three fundamental letters
            1. Up/down (Aleph)
            2. North/South (Shin)
            3. East/West (Mem)
3. Soul awareness
    1. This is awareness of the fundamental nature of a thing as limits begin to form around it.There are six dimension of soul awareness. This
        1. The 7 Double letters
            1. Center (Tau)
            2. Above (Beth)
            3. Below (Gimel)
            4. East (Daleth)
            5. West (Kaph)
            6. South (Resh)

7. North (Peh)

4. Physical awareness
    1. This is awareness and emanations of physical thing defined by its concrete form
        1. The twelve simple letters
            1. North East (Heh)
            2. South East (Vau)
            3. East Above (Zain)
            4. East Below (Cheth)
            5. North Above (Teth)
            6. North below (Yod)
            7. North Below (Lamed)
            8. South West (Nun)
            9. West Above (Samekh)
            10. West Below (Ayin)
            11. South Above (Tzaddi)
            12. South Below (Qoph)

3. Probability theory (calculated)(quantitative) (used to measure magic)

        1. The four worlds and probability
4. Doro: The ideal being for the practice
    1. Doro: A powerful being
        1. Doro is a character in Wild seed. He had the ability to possess other humans. Their soul is then booted out of their own body. This is a powerful ability, but in the novel Doro was limited. His existence is desirable for certain entities who enjoys being spirits and the pleasure of existing in a manu like form. I call this ability Genesis. A spirit that is in Malkuth develops his soul in such a way that it can attach itself to a "vessel," either at birth or maturity. If done at birth, the vessel is easier to control because a soul may not have entered or have claimed the body. So the body becomes the possession of the spirit, however the faculties of a human infant does not allow the spirit to fully merge with the body and function, and it would have to wait until the infant matures. It is for this reason partial Genesis is done, in which a part of the spirit is injected in the infants body, and a part remains in the astral world guiding the maturity of the body, until it is time to fully integrate. Full Genesis of an infant or undeveloped form is dangerous as the spirit has the potential to completely forget itself to the point where it has no compass of the spirit world: Full Genesis, however, is a teaching tool and training method of Yesodic beings, angels, and demons, and various spirits as it strengthens the spirit and teaches more about Key 0 .If the body is matured, a soul have already entered the body, and the spirit then

has to oveperpower the inhabitant of the body, or suppress the consciousness of the soul inhabiting the body. The success of this depends on the strength of the spirit performing Genesis and the strength of the soul/spirit inhabiting the body.

2. On the morality of Genesis: By the nature of Genesis, the act can be seen as a moral, however it is a practical and reasonable form of existence for a spirit that has no need for reincarnation, or has matured past the point of unstructured incarnation. Reincarnation is just another name for Full Genesis of a spirit/Soul . In Reincarnation the spirit seeks out a form that its soul vibrates too. If the spirit has matured to take on a manu form, it will seek out a manu form most suitable for its needs. After a while a soul becomes powerful enough where it can inhabit all sorts of manu forms. Such a soul may not want to fully incarnate because of the risk of forgetting itself.This is where Partial Genesis comes in. If a soul has developed to the point where it can inject its consciousness into a "vessel" without losing itself it has the right to do so. The topic of whether a spirit has the right to treat a body currently inhabited by a soul as a "vessel" is however up to debate as this act not only stealing but limits the growth of the soul in the body by forcing it out of incarnation. Yesodic beings hailing from angelic like planets respects the sanctuary of a soul in a body, and thus would only practice Partial Genesis of Infants, or Full Genesis of infants, and temporary Genesis on Mature bodies. Various demonic entities capable

of projecting their consciousness into a body disregards the moral nature of this.

3. Vessel Yoga considers the willingness of A spirit to see Genesis as a reasonable mode of existence and tool for growth. In the terms of inhabiting various bodies, we will call the act of consciously projecting your soul and spirit into another body possession. The alternative to this mode of existence that promotes the continuity of conscious existence (immortality) is physical immortality, or a perfected manu. the spirit is immortal by birthright but it is limited by its connection to the physical world. The soul and body is finite however. The soul is essentially vibrations of the spirit in connection to the physical world. This vibration is constantly moving unless the spirit directs it. This vibration is energy that is finite in the form that it presents itself in but can be reabsorbed. If the energy presents itself in a spirit form , when it dies out it turns into physical, thus the soul reincarnates into a body. If the energy presents itself in physical form, when it dies out the body dies and the soul returns to its spirit form. Now a perfected manu, which is not a manu that is human because humans are still limited a a manu form. A perfected Manu form has the ability of spirit recall from its conception. This allows the spirit to perfectly sit in the "vessel". This form is common amongst alien lifeforms. A perfected Manu form also has the ability or potential for bodily immortality. Because of this a Spirit can choose to inhabit a perfect manu form if its vibrations

and maturity allows it to. The downside of this is that Manu forms are considered heavy by mature spirits in the sense that being a spirit always allow a sense of freedom. Some perfected spirits choose this route for their existence. Some spirits perform Genesis of perfect Manu form and then learn and grow from that form, and put it to "Sleep" when necessary. Some spirits in the beginning are only able to inhabit a manu form, and then work on perfecting it into a perfect manu form.

2. Four Part soul and uniqueness of being human
    1. Akash of self and Akash of the outer Universe
3. The Steps of Magical Progression: An analysis of
    1. Step 1- Malkuth
        1. Meditation Basics
        2. The dimensional Key: Awareness Chakras of the Spirit,Soul, and body
        3. The Secret: Awareness of the two ultimate directions
    2. Step 2- Yesod
        1. Moving Awareness along the Chakras of Spirit, Soul and Body
        2. The Core practice: Developing a center
            1. Formlessness
            2. Imagination
            3. Dealing with Ashe/Prana/Chi
            4. The Secret
    3. Step 3- Hod
    4. Step 4- Netzach
    5. Step 5- Tiphareth
    6. Step 6- Geburah
    7. Step 7- Chesed

8. Step 8- Binah
9. Step 9- Chokmah
10. Step 10- Kether

4. Stages
    1. Assiah(Step 1- 2): Yoga
        1. Understanding of Your Nature and the Ultimate
            1. The distinction of Spirit, Soul,Body in the Yoga
                1. Sprit
                    1. Yoga aims to strengthen the imaginative capabilities of the Spirit. As it is immortal and a extension of Akasha. With a master of Key 0, an individual can work wonders with just this yoga. Mineral/ elemental stage. Elementals may choose to stay in this realm and become even more powerful elementals and master key 1 and 2 this way, with this path however they lose direct control of the physical world other than with their elemental forms. Or they may choose to become a Manu. In order to

advance in key 1 however they must develop some kind of physicality. Communication between Manu and elemental beings is only possible with either one of them utilizing key 2. It is easier for a Manu to bring a elemental to the physical plane, than it is for a elemental to bring a Manu to their plane or communicate with them. This is because the former is a condensation of Spirit, while the latter is a decondensation of Spirit. A true God is never really in a Manu form, unless it's an avatar incarnation, or a Doro like form. Lords have a Manu form, but usually keep it in their Underworld,as to bring that form to a middle world like earth would require a lot of work and knowledge, as such their Manu forms are astral in nature. Vegetative life is unique path that some elementals take, as vegetative life is a perfect physical counterpath to spirit, Though it is not the perfect tetrapolar magnet. Shamans usually utilize key 0 and this type of yoga to do amazing things

2. Soul
    1. The soul is your individuality. As such it is is fragile in the sense that it can be scattered and lost.With this in mind Yoga aims at strengthening the Existence of your individuality.The soul also is attached and integrated into the realm of Malkuth.So with direction of Spirit. KEY 0 and key 1 play a role in master of soul Yoga . In order to incarnate as a Man (the highest aspect of tetrapolar magnet for a spirit). You have to use Key 1. (Animal). Animal souls are

    usually elementals who are working on developing a Manu tetrapolar magnet. In the cycle of reincarnation they oscillate between their elemental and animal forms or vegetative. Another form of life that has the potential to rival animal, and become Manu are artificial In the form of technology.

3. Body
    1. The vessel to the spirit and the soul. In a hierarchy of difficulty of control. The spirit is the easiest to control, then the soul, and then the body. In the highest aspect of bodily Yoga, one would be able to regenerate body parts, shape shift, and mold the body like clay. This is easier done with the soul and body. The most an individual without mastery of the first Key (Key 1) can hope for is maintained it. This is one of

            the reasons that spirits choose to incarnate,it is so they master this key and Yoga. It is almost impossible to do it without an incarnation. (Manu). A key part in understanding physical yoga is understand what part of the modern is elemental/mineral, animal, and manu
        4. Take note of this: The major spiritual difference between an Elemental and a Manu IS that an elemental is part of a system and was ultimately created to work while Manu are created to have freedom from that system. A manu is a perfect Tetrapolar Magnet.
    2. The five limbed Yoga
        1. Asana
        2. Mudra
        3. Meditation
            1. Formlessness
            2. Imagination
        4. Ashe
        5. Purity
2. The Magical Art of Dreaming or Ala: A precursor to Astra-Physio magic
    1. The Four states of Awareness

1. Awake (In Physical and in Malkuth)
2. Daydreaming (Malkuth and Yesod)
3. Sleep-Death (Malkuthic sleep and Yesodic Sleep)
4. Dreaming (In Akashic self, In Malkuth, In Yesod, In Higher and Lower Planes)

2. The Three Yogic Practices of Dream Yoga or the Practice of Ala
   1. Meditation
      1. The technique and the Meditation symbol
         1. Forceful (Underworld)
         2. Natural (Middle World)
         3. Ultimate (Upperworld
   2. Ala-Lucid Dreaming
      1. The technique
         1. The Four Preparations
         2. The Four Main Practices (Chakra Based)
            1. Phase 1: Akasha to Air
            2. Phase 2: Air to Fire

            3. Phase 3: Fire to Water
            4. Phase 4: Water to Earth
    3. Projection- Traveling
        1. Dream Gates
            1. Gate 0- Day Dreaming
            2. Gate 1- Lucid Dreaming
            3. Gate 2- Dream travel
            4. Gate 3-Dream Mastery
            5. Gate 4- Spirit Projection/ Spirit travel
            6. Gate 5- Soul Projection/Soul travel
            7. Gate 6- Traveling
            8. Gate 7- Omnipresence
2. Yetzirah (Step 3-5): Tantra
    1. The applications or 8 vectors of magic: A precursor to higher forms of magic. The eight powers
        1. The vector of self
        2. The vector of other
        3. The vector of the past

            4. The vector of the future
            5. The vector of the UpperWorld
            6. The Vector of The Underworld
            7. The Vector of Parallel Self
            8. The Vector of Parallel Other
    3. Briah (Steps 6-7): Magic
        1. Magical Foundations
            1. The hidden name: The four part theory of magic
                1. Soul
                2. Structure
                3. Language
                4. Equation
    4. Atziluth (Steps 8-10): Divinity
5. The Tantric Magic : Limitless Possibilities of magic: Mudric Language
    1. The name
    2. A spell
    3. The Scroll
    4. The Tome
    5. An Arcanum

1. 1. 1.

35

The Magical Nature of Poetics and Story Mechanics

The Magical Nature of Poetics and Story Mechanics

1. In fool's poetics we saw that words and stories are portals. The Implications of this are strengthened with an understanding of mudric language.
2. A Verse is a tree and its roots. A Portal to a specific place within the six limits
3. The paths to the worlds of fiction and fantasy are through the underworld pass the mundane
4. Every story has layers corresponding to the Magical worlds
    1. Akashic world (Heart)
        1. Worlds Created by God's hands. Infinite
    2. Archetypal (Buddhic)
        1. Worlds that are possible by a divine mind
    3. Formative (Manasic)
        1. Worlds of existence

    2. It is here that we find actual worlds of fiction and fantasy
4. Creative (Pranic)
    1. Pranic worlds connected to this physics world. It is here we gain portals to different worlds of existence.
5. Material(Physicality)
    1. The material world that is common
    2. Language and Art are portals to such worlds

www.ingramcontent.com/pod-product-compliance
Lightning Source LLC
Chambersburg PA
CBHW050738150726
48196CB00003B/267
9798218489540